A New True Book

DANGEROUS FISH

By Ray Broekel

*This "true book" was prepared
under the direction of
Illa Podendorf,
formerly with the Laboratory School,
University of Chicago*

 CHILDRENS PRESS, CHICAGO

Tiger shark

PHOTO CREDITS

Miami Seaquarium—2, 4, (top), 9, 10, 12, 16, 17, 21, 34, 38, 39, 41

© Jeff Rotman—Cover, 4 (bottom), 6 (bottom), 14 (2 photos), 18, 22, 29, 30, 44

© A. Kerstitch—6 (top), 36

© James M. Cribb—43

Allan Roberts—7

James P. Rowan—24, 27, 32 (2 photos)

Cover—Sand Tiger Shark

The author studied, raised, and worked with fish for many years.

Library of Congress Cataloging in Publication Data

Broekel, Ray.
    Dangerous fish.

    (A New true book)
    Includes index.
    Summary: Photographs and brief text introduce piranhas, sharks, stonefish, electric catfish, and other dangerous marine animals.
    1. Dangerous fishes—Juvenile literature.
[1. Dangerous marine animals. 2. Marine animals] I. Title.
QL618.7.B76   597'.065   82-4464
ISBN 0-516-01635-0   AACR2

TABLE OF CONTENTS

Freshwater catfish

Puffer fish at night

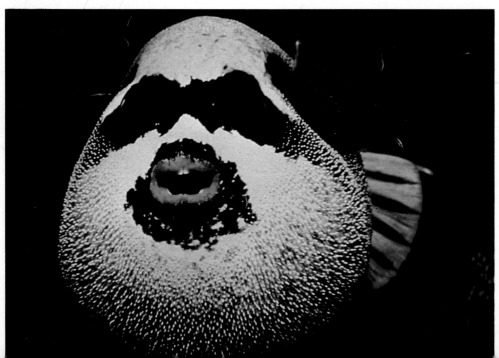

FISH

Some fish live in rivers, lakes, and ponds. They are called freshwater fish.

Other fish live in the oceans. They are called saltwater fish.

Most kinds of fish are not dangerous to people.

But some kinds can be dangerous.

You will meet the dangerous fish in this book.

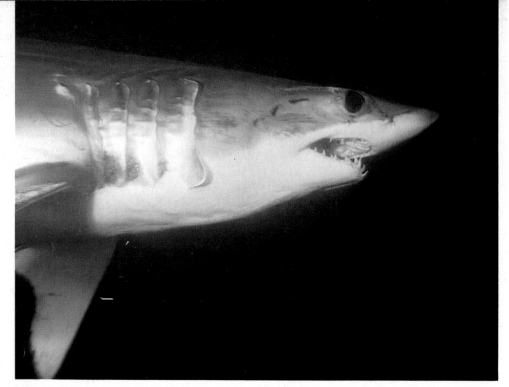

Mako shark

Reef shark in the Red Sea

Leopard shark

SHARKS

There are over 250 kinds of sharks. Only about a dozen kinds have attacked people.

One dangerous kind is the mako. This shark is about eleven feet long.

Another kind is the great white shark. It attacks and eats almost anything.

A great white shark may be as long as thirty-six feet.

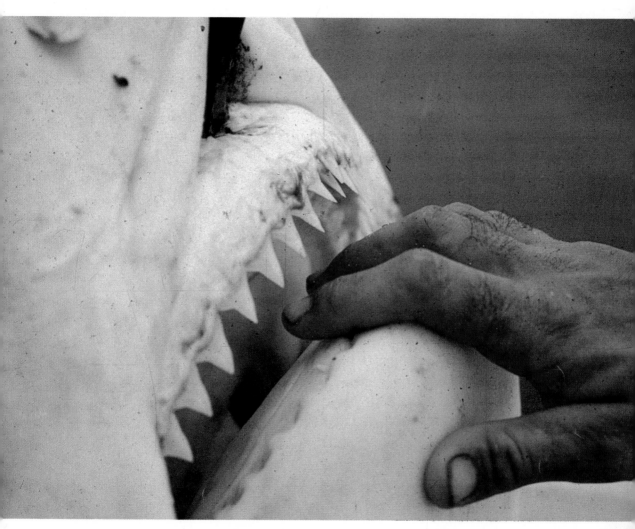

Close-up of shark teeth

9

Hammerhead shark

The hammerhead is a strange-looking shark. It has a flat, spread head. It reaches a length of about sixteen feet.

The hammerhead can be a mean and dangerous shark.

Shark, eating fish

A shark swims towards things making unusual noises in the water. A splashing swimmer makes such a noise.

A shark has a good sense of smell. It can smell blood almost half a mile away.

Tiger shark (above) and jaws of fifteen-foot tiger shark (below)

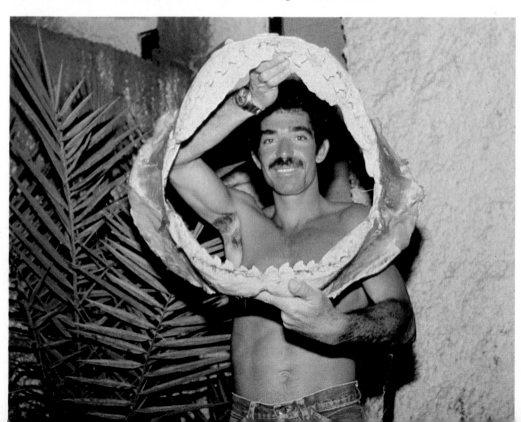

Tiger sharks are about eighteen feet long.

Dusky sharks are about eleven feet long.

Both these sharks are dangerous.

Some sharks lay eggs. Most kinds have their young alive.

A baby shark is called a pup. A pup is born with teeth, so it is ready to fight and bite.

Young tiger shark

Lemon shark

The lemon shark is about nine feet long.

The blue shark is longer. It may be from nine to twelve feet.

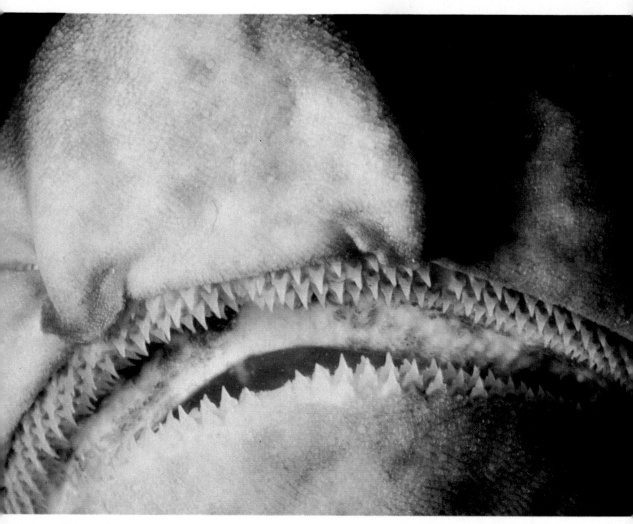

Rows of teeth in a swell shark

A shark does not need to turn over to bite. The lower jaw is pushed forward. Then the shark bites with the teeth in both jaws.

A shark's teeth are sharp. And there are plenty of them.

Most sharks live in the oceans. But one kind lives in freshwater.

It lives in a lake. This lake is in Nicaragua, Central America. The shark is called the bull, or Lake Nicaragua, shark.

This shark grows to be about eight feet long. It has bitten and even killed people in the lake.

BARRACUDAS

Barracudas are found in the oceans.

One kind, the giant barracuda, grows to be about six feet long.

21

Barracuda in the Red Sea

The Pacific barracuda is about four feet long.

These two kinds are dangerous. Other kinds are not.

A barracuda uses sight to find something to eat.

It rests quietly in the water. When the barracuda sees something moving, it checks to see what it is. Then the barracuda takes one quick bite.

The bite is a big one. A barracuda has a mouth full of teeth.

Lionfish

THE LIONFISH

The lionfish has many brightly-colored fins. It is also known as the turkey fish. It lives in tropical ocean waters.

Inside each brightly-colored fin is a sharp spine. Poison is shot out when a spine is touched. The wound can be very painful.

THE STONEFISH

The stonefish is very ugly. It is the most poisonous fish in the world. The stonefish shoots poison out through its spines.

The stonefish lives in the South Pacific and Indian oceans. It lives on ocean bottoms near the shore.

Stonefish

CALIFORNIA
SCORPION FISH

The California scorpion fish gives off a poison from some of its fin spines.

This fish is found in the oceans off California.

Scorpion fish

Close-up of the poisonous spines on a scorpion fish

People who fish, often catch scorpion fish. They must be careful taking this fish off their hook. Unless care is taken, they may get a painful wound.

Green moray eel (above) and spotted moray eel (below)

MORAY EELS

Moray eels are often found in ocean coral reefs. They have strong jaws and sharp teeth. They are about six feet long.

Morays are dangerous when they are bothered. They strike out like snakes when they bite. Their bites are not poisonous.

Electric eel

ELECTRIC EELS

Electric eels live in fresh water in South America. They can give off electric shocks.

Sometimes people brush against an electric eel by accident. The people can be knocked unconscious. The electric shocks are very strong.

Electric ray

ELECTRIC RAYS

Rays live in the oceans.
Some kinds of rays give
off electric shocks if
touched.

Some rays are very
small. Others may be as
large as six feet across.

STINGRAYS

Some kinds of rays are stingrays. They have stingers in their tails.

The stingers are sharp spines. They are poisonous. The stings can be very painful.

Atlantic stingray

Most stingrays live in the oceans.

A few freshwater rays live in South America.

Some kinds of stingrays are about seven feet long.

Electric catfish from Africa

ELECTRIC CATFISH

The electric catfish lives in fresh water. It is found in Africa.

The electric catfish is about four feet long. It gives off electric shocks to capture its food.

It will also use electric shocks against its enemies.

PIRANHAS

Piranhas are small fish. Most kinds are no longer than one foot.

Piranhas are found in South America. They live in rivers.

Many kinds of piranhas are dangerous.

Why are piranhas dangerous?

Piranha

Piranhas have very sharp teeth. They also have strong jaws. Piranhas can take a nasty bite.

Piranhas swim in groups. There may be hundreds in the group. The smell of blood makes them bite.

Each piranha in the group takes a bite. That's why piranhas are so dangerous.

Wolf eel

DANGEROUS FISH

You have read about some dangerous fish. Now would you like to see some of them?

Moray eel

Where would be a safe place?

Visit a public aquarium. That way the fish can look at you, too.

WORDS YOU SHOULD KNOW

aquarium(ah • KWAIR • ee • yum) — a building where fish and other animals are kept.

attack(ah • TACK) — to set upon with angry force.

capture(CAP • cher) — to catch; to get hold of.

coral(KORE • ul) — a hard substance that is formed by the skeltons of sea animals.

dangerous(DAIN • jer • us) — full of harm; risky.

enemy(EN • ih • mee) — not a friend.

Nicaragua(nick • ah • RAH • gwah) — a country in Central America.

reef — a strip of coral at or near the surface of a body of water.

tropical(TROP • ih • cul) — hot and humid.

unconscious(un • CAHN • shuss) — not aware; a condition that looks like sleep.

wound(WOOND) — an injury.

INDEX

About the Author

Ray Broekel is a full-time freelance writer who lives with his wife, Peg, and a dog, Fergus, in Ipswich, Massachusetts. He has had twenty years of experience as a children's book editor and newspaper supervisor, and has taught all subjects in kindergarten through college levels. Dr. Broekel has had over 1,000 stories and articles published, and over 100 books. His first book was published in 1956 (it was published by Childrens Press).